EMPTY ROOM
WITH LIGHT

EMPTY ROOM
WITH LIGHT

Poems

Ann Hostetler

DreamSeeker Books
TELFORD, PENNSYLVANIA

an imprint of
Pandora Press U.S.

Copublished with
Herald Press
Scottdale, Pennsylvania

Pandora Press U.S. orders, information, reprint permissions:
pandoraus@netreach.net
1-215-723-9125
126 Klingerman Road, Telford PA 18969
www.PandoraPressUS.com

Grateful acknowledgement is made to the
editors of the publications in which the following poems first appeared:
American Scholar: Painting with My Daughter, Resisting Geometry; *The
Aurorean*: Thumbelina; *Cream City Review:* Improvisations; *DreamSeeker
Magazine:* Apparition; *Espresso Poetry:* Geese; *Greeting the Dawn:* Spareribs;
Kairos: Walnut Tree, Insomnia; *Mankato Poetry Review:* Properties of Objects;
The Mid-America Poetry Review: Female Ancestor; *The Mennonite:* Family
Portrait (Holy Family), The Iconoclast; *Mothering:* Looking at Pictures With
My Mother, Marriage With Children; *Porcupine:* Errand.

Library of Congress Cataloguing-in-Publication Data
Hostetler, Ann Elizabeth.
Empty room with light : poems / Ann Hostetler
p. c.m.
ISBN 1-931038-10-4 (Alk. paper)
1. Mennonites--Poetry. 2. Family--Poetry. 3. Woment--Poetry. I. Title
PS3608.O53 E4 2002
811'.6--dc21
2002029959

10 09 08 07 06 05 04 03 02   10 9 8 7 6 5 4 3 2 1

To
my mother

Contents

BOOK ONE
Impressions

Looking at Pictures with my Mother

We turned the pages again and again
in the quiet times when my sister slept
and you were mine alone,
my cheek resting against your
cotton shirtwaist,
the heavy book in your lap.
I can still remember the grain
of the dark blue fabric cover
opening onto the flesh tones
and red accents
of Renoir. Lush, full,
the white-skinned bathers
were my favorites,
their bodies poised in and out of water,
naked women reclining and talking
in familiar clusters,
as when I knelt beside the tub
and traced the surface of your bath water
with my fingertips, posing as your equal,
the woman I hoped to become.

Iconoclast

My grandfather Ezra painted a gigantic face
on the side of the shed when he cleaned his brushes,
stroking the weathered boards with leftover barn red,
till a man with worldly mustache and pompadour

stared out across his half-section of Alberta wheat.
Ezra himself kept the Ordnung, shaved his mustache
and trimmed his beard, though he played baseball
on Saturdays. Nothing wrong with a little fun.

But a newcomer moved in down the road,
complained that his neighbor had painted a pinko
for everyone to see. Ezra shrugged, whitewashed the shed,
returned to the plow with a book in his hand.

No matter if the furrows are crooked, he said,
the seed will sprout just the same.
And Sundays after church he drew eagles
in the margins of his Bible.

The Anarchist

All I wanted was to create
something new with heat and light—
something that had never been seen.

Focusing the acetylene torch
on the reddening steel, I destroyed
straight lines, dross clumping

like candle wax as I carved
scrap metal into a surprising lace.
I wondered how the guys

in my otherwise all-male sculpture class
could stay content perfecting
hidden seams, matching straight

edges at right angles, replicating
cubes and pyramids, forms
so public and so crafted.

Female Ancestor

for Irene, whom I never met

A farm woman opens
the oven door of the coal stove
to stir the embers, re-latches
the door with a cast iron tool, sets
it down, wipes her hands, moves
to the sink where she bends
to peel and soak potatoes. She turns
to wipe down the oil cloth,
unbottle pickled beets
into the blue glass dish passed down
from her grandmother.
After the meal she bends over
the sink, scrapes and washes
crusted pots, feeds scraps
to the dog. Her daughter dries
and puts the dishes away.

For decades the woman bends
over washing, over mending.
She hangs out the heavy sheets,
bends over ironing, over tubs
of water drawn from the cistern
and heated for baths.
She bends with sleepy children
over their school books,
bends over their fever-flushed
faces. Twice she bends over
a tiny coffin. She bends
over her husband's back,
her veined, callused hands
kneading his work-hardened
muscles. Before she dies

she cuts down one of his suits,
hums as she bends over to sew a traveling
outfit for her daughter's trip to college,
the long train ride that will
separate them forever.

Muse

Walking through the last stretch
of virgin prairie in Northern Illinois, I listen
to her voice musing on a daughter, still unconceived,
who will wear the baby dresses her mother's
been sewing and folding away in tissue.
Her thick, dark, wavy hair parts in the breeze,
her strong jaw sets itself against the almost
white sky, pregnant with Autumn light,
brooding over goldenrod, withered blackberries,
budding asters swollen with summer's
last blooms. My friend and I walk in the place
where paintings are painted, poems are made,
where thoughts swill in the quiescent air,
then settle like pollen over the fertile brain.
She is in residence for a month, I am only
visiting for a few hours, my children at home
with a sitter they don't like
as I walk beside her and listen
to that daughter question, our words
like seeds, scattered on densely
thicketed earth.

Thumbelina

Beneath the rosy shade
of a dogwood in fall bloom
I awake, curled in your palm.
Light filters through the single leaf
you hold above me. Together we
examine its mottled surface: you see
the downy, opaque, underside.
I see ribs drawn dark
like spokes of an umbrella
against luminescent flesh,
shielding me from the revelation of your face,
creased valleys on either side
of your mouth, shaded hollows
beneath your lashes,
the liquid glassy surface
of your eyes reflecting a tiny girl-shaped
speck of light.

Father

In the bookstore a tall blonde man
with long eyelashes and transparent
skin stoops to meet the whispers
of his tiny dark-haired daughter.
His listening brings out the blue
in his eyes, the tender lines
around his mouth, as salt brings out
the flavor of food.

The Walnut Tree

From my swing I gazed
upward into a universe of leaves
(the sweep of ground beneath my feet
scuffed bare), a branching abundance
that sheltered me.

Against the concrete walk
I crushed the casings
of green nuts that dropped from the tree
and rotted on the lawn, my fierce heels
cracking the tougher shells
like ribs, like the things I hated.

Each time I taste
a walnut fresh as those that fell
from the aging tree in our back yard
I remember how I broke the shells,
dug out the firm white meat and
savored it against my tongue.

The Easter Coat

I woke with a dull ache—deeper
but less painful than a normal stomachache—
nausea somewhat less than carsickness, the rust
stain on my faintly flowered Carter's Spanky Pants
almost a kind of disappointment after all the preparation:
pads laid out carefully by my mother, then tucked
away for me in the linen closet, the elastic
sanitary belt she'd asked me to try on as though
it were a new garment. Sitting on the toilet
I remembered the Kotex booklet they'd given
us at school: *You may be more concerned now*
about the styles and colors you wear. You begin
to develop a taste in clothing that is your own.
This style may be different from your mother's.
That very same day my mother picked up a "find"
at the bargain fabric store—the softest wool
I'd ever touched, in a woven plaid of silvery olive,
peach, and ivory—something a grown woman
might wear. At home she held its colors up
to my face and said, "Let's make a coat for you
to celebrate your becoming a woman."
I don't know whether I even thanked her,
but held myself stiff with embarrassment,
as when, next day at school, still a child,
I stood in the cafeteria line between two boys
jostling devil's horns behind each other's heads,
fearing I'd bleed through the yellow dotted swiss
organdy dress (with its ridiculous little-girl sash)
inherited from my neighbor's teen-aged cousin,
thinking of the coat my mother would sew me,
how its sophisticated pastel plaid
would cover me in the pooling April rains
as I waited for the fragrant, blossoming spring
I'd vaguely imagined all winter.

Compromise

When I followed my parents through museums
I vowed I would never own anything I couldn't make
by hand. I would study weaving and embroidery,
spin flax and wool, learn carpentry with the hand-hewn tools
I saw behind display case glass—their wooden handles
smoothed by users' palms—grow vegetables
and gather dyes from wild plants.
Cars were out. And television, too,
At least until I understood physics,
mechanical engineering, electricity.
Without radio or hi fi I would make my own
music, dip candles for light, melt
fat and lye for soap. I quailed
at the thought of butchering, though.
I'd have to go vegetarian.
As I thought about the simple life
I would choose—using only things
I could make from scratch—I realized
I would have to take the lives of trees
to build my house, dislodge
stones from their earthly resting place
to line the cellar. Undaunted, I planned
orchards and gardens, until I realized
that even the lettuce would have to die
to sustain me. By the time we stopped
at Howard Johnson's on the car ride home
I decided I wouldn't begin just yet,
that one more hamburger,
one more trip in the family car,
wouldn't hurt, that some day, in the far
distant future, I would find a way
to live life on its own terms.

Still Life

In Aunt Lizzie's Old Order home
color was meaning—unmixed as jewel tones

in a child's paint box. Every combination
had its boundaries, as red beet eggs,

when sliced, showed distinct concentric rings
of magenta, pink, white, and yellow.

In the parlor forest green window shades
shielded from too much light the family Bible

that lay open on the folded drop-leaf table
covered by a blue and white-checked cloth

beneath the shiny autumn scene on the 1954
calendar from Zook's general store. Rocking

chairs of different shapes and sizes circled
the room, their patterned cushions made by hand,

worked in winter leisure in velveteen patchwork
or crewel yarns. On weekdays only the clattering

thunder of the marble roller broke the silence
in that room, when we came to visit and the grown-ups

gathered in the barn or kitchen to talk about important things.
In the close-cropped yard pansies bloomed

inside whitewashed tractor tires, the ones an Amish farmer
must discard, replace with steel wheels.

Aunt Lizzie once told us the pansies had faces.
My sisters and I imagined them Old Order, their colors

wine-dark as the shades of women's dresses. Sometimes
the women stopped by the yard and looked on, smiling, as we
played.

Resisting Geometry

The first time I saw my father defeated
he was leaving the only parent-teacher conference
he ever had concerning my academic failure,
his black raincoat drooping over one arm.
Settling his other arm over my shoulder,
he walked me to the car, told me about
his sixth-grade failure to master fractions.

How could I explain to him
it was the axioms themselves
I objected to, knowing that, like his whims,
I had to take them on faith.
Tested against experience
they appeared to be correct—
no two points could occupy the same space
at the same time; lines perfectly parallel
will never intersect; a straight line
is the shortest distance between two points.
But such self-evidence troubled me.

Imagining exceptions, I felt called
To test the axioms, to wage a battle
against givens, resisting at the root.
When the boys circled Mr. Oelkers
at the blackboard, arguing logic,
I sat at the back of the room
drawing shapes that defied these laws.

It was only in the spring, sprawled out
in front of the stereo, listening to James Taylor
and embroidering the margins of my geometry book
with blue ball-point pen, that I discovered
what was at stake for me was the axiomatic quality

of reasoning itself, the ways in which our assumptions
construct reality, become paradigms
that organize our vision.

I realized that no one else took geometry
as seriously as I did—at least no one
who was failing, that is—and that
in order to get on with life
I would have to get beyond axioms,
memorize theorems, prove hypotheses.

This was not art, where my doodles
might have some eccentric meaning.
This was a game with rules
and if I put aside my distrust of logic
long enough, I could learn to play.
But there was no longer time
to be good at it, only time to garner
a hard-won D.

When the final report came home
I tried to explain my triumph to my father—
my passing as an act of will—
that at the last minute
I had mastered something more
than grades reflected. As I began
to speak a shadow settled over his face.
Even at fourteen I saw that he was weighing
how much he could take on faith.

The Way Out

My grandfather Ezra never made much
as a farmer, the depression nearly foreclosing
on his father's legacy—a half section of land
he'd mortgaged to buy another half section
he could never pay off. So he read as he plowed
crooked furrows, studied Revelation, drew elegant stylized
birds and diagrams in the margins of
his Bible study pamphlets solved puzzles
in *The Grain Grower's Guide* till he won
the only new car he ever owned—'tata, 'tata, 'tata—
my mother imitated the sound it made crossing
rutted Alberta roads when it carried the family
to church twice each Sunday.

> *I'd try to fall asleep on the back seat*
> *on the way home so I could be carried in. They'd ask,*
> *"Little Beulah, are you asleep?"*
> *And I'd say, "Yes."*

Little by little the Overland Whippet Touring car
began to carry him away—across vast flat sections of wheat
for weeks at a time to teach Winter Bible School.

> *We were there with only mother and the hired man*
> *so we had to dig 'taters till our finger bones ached, almost*
> *every meal was made from 'taters Mother fried with lard*
> *and onions. 'Taters huge as dinosaur eggs*
> *that Father argued with our Creationist schoolteacher*
> *could have existed because the Bible says,*
> *"The earth* became *without form and void."*

None of his children live in that place any more
and none of his land is theirs—they all drove away

when they got old enough for wheels.
Before the old home place was sold I'd ride
there in the back seat of my parents' car:

"When will we get there?
When will we get there?"

lulled to sleep by the hum
of the dark paved road.

BOOK TWO

Family Gallery

Lullaby

I rock you and sing to you,
little one who will not go to sleep.
Your hungry gaze, direct
and unsmiling, meets mine.
I work through all the songs I know
as they occur to me: *Summertime,*
Today while the Blossoms, Oh Nobody
Knows the Trouble I've Seen trying
to get you to give up your hold
on the world for even an hour.
Sometimes I Feel like a Motherless Child,
especially when I realize you see
through me—
my impatience, my need
to be released.

Holy Family

In Giotto's *Nativity*
angels and shepherds look
outwards or upwards,
while the swaddled
newborn holds his head up
to peer into his mother's eyes.
Who sees the other more clearly—the serene
reclining mother an intimate arm's length
from God? Or her son
whose perfectly formed doll's face
welcomes the eyes of the one
who brought him forth from her body?
Already he knows her labor pains, her joy
at his head crowning between
her legs, the weary journey. Her centuries'
worn blue robe, crumbling and translucent,
joins her to the almost sleeping Joseph
folded in a fetal squat
beside the clustered rams.

The Properties of Objects

She shows me the properties of objects:
the ringing cylinder of copper-bottomed
stainless steel, the perfect fit and clang
of its lid. The yellowed wood of a mixing spoon
yields to her new teeth. Nesting cups
are for lightness and shiver, salty tang
of aluminum pressed against raw gum.
Time and space are consonants buzzing
about her ears as the world swirls out
from the patterned linoleum
firmly fixed beneath
her patting hands.

Improvisations

How I miss those times when I could make
a fool of myself folding laundry,
shaking out clean, dry diapers
so I could hide my face,
then peek out at you, sing
loudly and recklessly anything
that came to mind, making up forgotten lines:

Tyger, tyger burning bright
in deep forests of delight—

or

Dark brown is the river
where my thoughts like golden sand
flow along forever from my head
into your hands—

You'd tilt your face towards mine
and grin from the blanket
where you sat Buddha-like
sorting a jumble of toys
from one basket to another,
already showing me the order
with which you apprehended
the chaos of family living,
while I fumbled through undershirts and towels
searching for rhymes from childhood,
worn-out memories patched
with moments of invention.

Painting with my Daughter
We wet the dry discs,
soak the brushes in ultra tones—
royal blue,
magenta, aquamarine—
wisps of brush stroking
mark the thick paper,
the silence,
faint inrush of breath
when the world runs together
making volcanoes of color
in the early shadows of November afternoon.

After we finish
I stand before the window
flushing out the pigments
at the kitchen sink,
red and blue bleeding from the brushes
into the stream of clear water.
I hear her singing to herself
in the next room,
already caught up
in something new.

I do not turn on the light
but stand as shadow thickens
objects around me,
the window before me a square of fading light,
framing bare branches,
a frozen garden,
the cracked blue plastic swimming pool
from last summer.

Marriage, with Children

Once we made love everywhere—
curve of your flank
fitted to mine
on blankets, grass,
the wool rug in my parents' den,
standing in a mosquito-infested field.
Love of youth so hungry for its own
expansion, enamored of its power
to arouse, to be aroused,
rollicking, teasing, melting
love slippery as words.

Now years of living together
have pinned us down,
pinned me under, grinding wheat
between stones each morning
as you hoist your attache case
like the caveman his club,
off hunting. I tend
countless lists: groceries,
appointments, school trips,
doctor's visits, phone messages—
I'm sorry he's not here—

"Mommy I want to crawl back inside you
again," says the one who is three.
And the baby clings, squalling
to pull me from his sister.
My arms ache. We all await
your key in the door.

As the kids tease your weary smile
I close my eyes, feel our marriage falling

like a loose, baggy net about us.
Then your thumbs press
against my spine.
I ease into your touch,
a moment's elasticity.
As your fingers work the muscles
of my back, our life draws taut again,
a web hung rich with glittering complexity,
unimagined in our youthful love.

Bonding

for Ted Cheek

Birth was attended by the men in green:
my husband, you, and two plump students.
"The three stooges!" I cried.
When you crowded into the labor room
I snapped a photograph.

I'd wanted to do it naturally,
but the baby would not descend.
Instead they sent for you
to explain the procedure
that would numb the feeling.

Behind my back your hands
find the space in my spine
where the needle will go.
"Forget what you've read now,
and let your fingers
lead you to the place,"
you tell the interns,
reading the map of the vertebrae,
a musician finding a note
on the neck of his instrument.
I feel your knowing touch,
then the numbing pinch,
dull pressing of the catheter
squeaking through cartilage
like styrofoam
to that elusive
epidural space.

Heavy nerve-sleep creeps
across my belly,

spreads down to distant toes.
Covered with sheets, my belly
shielded from my view,
I feel a tug, then hear a sudden cry.
Unclasping my hand to watch
his son being born, my husband disappears
behind the drape.

But you know I need to touch someone
Your soft large hand
now calmly presses mine.

"You're the first father
I ever heard sing in surgery,"
I hear you say. My husband's
voice floats in to my ear, crooning
lullabies to rhythmic cries.
You take back your hand.

My husband places the infant
bundle in my arms, the miracle
we have all been waiting for, and you
pick up the abandoned camera
to take a photograph:
the three of us embracing,
united by your discreetly
hidden eye.

Inside the Lines

Across the table in a restaurant
he takes up a fresh crayon,
moves the red tip inside
the outlines of a snowman
on a page torn from a coloring book.
He is three and I have never shown him
how to color inside the lines.
He tells me to watch and I do,
admiring the lace-work of his strokes.
"Can you color his carrot nose?"
He finally offers me a job: mixing
red and yellow—like mustard and catsup.
The waxy hues blend unevenly.
I return the crayon, and he
hands me another,
begs me to join him once more
inside the printed lines.

Chore

Dressed for basketball practice
in blue nylon shorts and high tops, my son
volunteers to do the ironing. From the stack
of wrinkled laundry he pulls the colored squares
of napkins and smoothes them over the padded
board while I carefully pour distilled water
into the heating steel triangle that has fascinated
him since he was nicked by it as a toddler.
Steam hisses as he reaches for the handle
with one hand, uncurls the corners of the fabric
with the other. I notice his plump fingers are growing
swiftly to man size. As I heat up leftover spaghetti
and chicken nuggets for supper, the warm
pressed squares of cloth appear on the countertop
one after the other like prayer flags, then reappear
as neatly folded triangles beneath the forks
on the kitchen table.

Errand

Beside me in the blue Toyota van
you lean against the seat and stare
at the billboards, at the sunset

silently taking the world into
your mind in what proportions
I can only guess—does the Marlboro

cowboy looming before us color
your thoughts since you have seen
the movies that explain his lung cancer

death, or do you look beyond obstructions
to the purpling horizon, miniature pines
and dark houses, marking the place where

the earth curves out of sight? At the periphery
of my vision I am aware of your nine-year-old
body in jeans and baseball cap, freckled cheeks

and luminous dark eyes full and remote
as twin planets, as time's shadow
falling between us.

Fast Food

One hand against the vinyl-covered steering wheel,
the other warmed with soft bread, I bite
into a mixture of creamy condiments,
wilted lettuce, fatty grilled meat handed
to me in a paper box through the sliding glass,
then seized and plundered.

In the back seat the kids open up the nuggets,
grab fistfulls of fries, lay the salted
leather strips—barely warm—
against their tongues in the dark
mouth of the car. The tremor

of raw hunger slaked seizes us
on the highway home. Signaling
to switch lanes past other moving cars,
other sealed containers, I taste another
bite and another, not asking what I eat

or where it comes from, only that steam
fill my nostrils and that the kids' whining
be muffled by chewing, that we be
satisfied before we spill out
into the empty house.

Teething

"It has been a moral teething." —Emily Bronte

For months your have fastened
your tiny moist mouth around my
aureole, tongue and gums drawing out
all the milk you can hold. Droplets run
across your plump cheeks as you stretch
the nipple, then pull away, sated, turn
immediately to other oral satisfactions—
measuring spoons and bits of toast,
paper, wooden blocks, and plastic rings,
my nose, cheeks, and hair, which you grasp
firmly and press to your gently puckered lips—
open to the world and taking it all in. Now
something has come between us:
a slim bit of razor-sharp ivory edging upwards
from beneath the irritated welts of your gums,
a dangerous seed sprouting as a spear
that craves resistance. I will never
again trust your sucking completely now that you
have gnawed your way through necessary pain.

Geese with Their Young

She tugs my finger and tilts
her curly head, front teeth meeting
in an open smile, then parting slightly
to her tongue hissing new words:
"Geese? Geese?"
How can I refuse to follow
as she tugs my hand and pulls me towards
the pond. I know she is imagining
the graceful birds we saw there yesterday
at dusk. We climb through a grove of spruce
to the place where memory meets her
in the shape of geese, paired and floating
with their young. We sit on the concrete spillway
and watch the geese float in each others' company.
It is only moments until she backs into
my lap, lowers herself in my arms,
turns, laughing 'night 'night.
I lift my shirt,
her hands cup my breast,
her busy sucking echoes
the distant conversation
of geese with their young.

Daughter, Age 9

She lunges though the screen door
to stop us from pruning the overgrown
spirea, hangs on her father's arm
with all her furious weight to keep him
from digging out the prickly, choking juniper:
"You're killing something green!"
"You're killing something green!"

After school I find her arguing
with her third grade teacher:
"We shouldn't build any more bridges.
We shouldn't build any more roads.
We shouldn't build any more houses.
We shouldn't build any more factories.
We can ride horses or bikes.
We can grow all our food.
We can share the houses we have.
We can use our hands to make things."

Her pockets are full of acorns,
her socks filled with pebbles,
her permanent teeth stained with chocolate.
I dare not disturb sacred piles
of dried eggshells, bird nests, seedpods,
colored foil wrappers. Alone on the back porch
she wraps herself in flower chains
and sarongs of uncut calico, makes prayer
bundles of dried flowers, beads, stones
in the antique handkerchiefs I passed on
to her from my own childhood.

When she dresses to go out
she ties on a long apron and a shawl,

answers the call of the mourning dove,
cradles earthworms in her palms,
walks into the rain with open, upturned mouth,
brings me toast and tea in bed,
lives stories
I've all but forgotten.

Elegy for a Babysitter

I.

Through the screen door
her pale red hair, flecked with dried grass,
fanned about her made-up face. She was sorry,
she said, that she looked so awful now,
straightening her dark green dress,
shaking the button on her jacket
that declared "smoking stinks."
When I opened the door
scents of tobacco and doublemint
followed in her wake. I left
uneasily, hurried back as quickly as I could.

II.

Before I met Jenny, her mother
introduced herself, confided
she wrote poetry. "Jenny's different.
I wish someone could understand her."
Did I know where she could publish it?

III.

A neighbor calls to tell me that Jenny died
last night in her driveway, next to ours,
and asks me what I know. Nothing
save the echoes of last night's game
of "kick the can" ringing in my ears,
a remembrance of hurrying my kids off to bed.

IV.

Finally I hear how it happened.
The game over, she clowned from the window
of her boyfriend's car, begged him
to back down the drive. She lost

her balance, hit her head,
stumbled to her feet
and walked into the house.
She had no idea this was it.

V.

Tonight I cannot sleep.
I rise and see from my bedroom window
the family room of her home,
illuminated through an arched window,
her father sitting alone on the couch,
arms crossed and folded to his chest.
A telescope stands scaffold-like before the glass.
No one there is looking at the stars tonight.

VI.

In the kitchen I discover
A plastic container she'd brought me
when I borrowed eggs for brownies.
Is it for this bit of unfinished
business that her body projects
its images everywhere in the house,
always at the periphery of vision,
especially when I wake and stumble
to my children's darkened rooms
and listen for their breathing?

Coda:

Memories of our first meeting flood
back to me, what I saw as her confusion
so vividly before me. Somehow I hold myself
responsible, mourn this loss—her life
gone before she could begin to unravel
that tangle of emotions she thought
roped her so securely to this earth.

Transformations

Julia waves her magic wand
and changes from Cinderella
into one of the wicked stepsisters.
"My name is Anastasia," she crows,
"and I want to rip my sister's party dress."
Already at three she's discovered
the advantage in playing all the roles—
you can't do much as Cinderella
without a prince or fairy godmother,
and pretending to be wicked
is just plain fun.
With her auburn ringlets,
her passion for kisses and crinolines,
she'll need her own magic
slippers, a range that can take her
anywhere, transformations
she can work herself.

Julia Packs Up Her Playthings

Stuffed into the blue plastic case
left over from my sister's childhood—
when they only came with brunette or blond hair
and peach-colored plastic skin
(even the red-head was given a different
name: Midge)—my daughter's Barbies peer out
from beneath ruffled skirts and frizzed
acrylic hair—Beach Party Barbie, Quinceañera
Barbie, Dutch Barbie, Swedish Barbie, Slumber Party
Barbie, Native American Barbie, Pocahontas
and Nokomis with slim Barbie legs and cone-
shaped breasts, Tropical Splash Barbie, African-
American Barbie, Christmas 1993 Barbie
in her green velveteen gown, Career Barbie,
Casey and Pizza Hut Skipper
and one of the smaller Madelines—
a daycare center full of Barbies—
all wearing each others'
clothes or none at all, packed up
at the end of the day with play-stained
disco gowns and bathing suits, extra
socks, paired with best friends, micro-
scopic Polly Pocket dolls caught in mismatched
Barbie mules—feet sticking in the face
of an enemy who said they didn't
chew snack with their mouth
shut, or who wouldn't let them
play house.

She clicks the latch,
lifts the plastic handle,

waves to me as I type
at my PC.

See you later, dearie.
I'm off to work.

On Loaning Maternity Clothes to a Friend

I nestle fabrics
I've almost forgotten wearing
into cardboard boxes, eager
to hasten the comfort of a friend, enhance
her pleasure in awaiting her unborn
child. As I fold them I imagine wearing them again:
a cotton shift of sea-green tinged with nausea,
a sweater the deep blue of clear water,
a top and skirt finely striped black and white
like the horizontal pattern on a blank television
screen awaiting a face, a voice
as yet untuned. That once awaited child
is walking everywhere now, chattering,
doing deep knee bends, chuckling
at her own antics, feeding and hugging
her dolls. Until now I'd almost forgotten
the caress of these cottons and silks on my skin,
the feel of my body thickening,
into its own soft armor,
her being swelling inside me.

Empty Room, with Light
for David

Today we sold the house you were born in,
your room with lilac walls so pale
they formed only the faintest ice-cream
shadow against white woodwork
and window frames opening onto
a sea of green grass and maple leaves.

One last time we cross sun-streaked
floor boards—you hold my hand
and walk now—empty of your crib,
the day bed where I slept to comfort you
at night, the desk where I wrote down what I felt
and saw your first few snowy months on earth.

Stripped of our possessions, that room still holds
a quality of light I will carry with me, illuminating
my dense unseeing heart, blood-pump that one day
will cause me to sink beneath this cluttered life
into the green world outside the window
where sun now softly filters through the leaves.

BOOK THREE
Life Studies

Thistles

Mid-July thistles bloom on roadside banks
in shades of lavender, purple, bruise,
nodding flirtatious heads, foliage
armored against uprooting. With leather-gloved
hands I have yanked them from the hard clay
of my Wisconsin garden, yet they rise up again
eager for survival. Sometimes I ask myself
whether I should let them flower. No.
They would scatter their seeds everywhere.
Still, I love to see them bloom on distant
hillsides I'm not responsible for weeding,
revel in the deep hues of their tasseled petals
as I pass them on the freeway in an air-
conditioned mini-van, the kids
squabbling in the back.

Leafy

On our walks you stoop to pick up
young oak leaves with loopy cartoon
cut-out shapes, or discover details—
a praying mantis on a crumbling wall.
I look down at your graying sneakers
and see cream-colored cobbles, rose
blush of brick shaped by the slender curve
of the insect's yellow-green body.
In *The Hungry Mind* we sit shoulder
to shoulder on the worn canvas sofa
as you show me the slate, stick, and leaf
constructions of Andy Goldsworthy in their slick
papered photographic art-book splendor.
I want to turn and look at you, tell you
how you make me see things—your eyes
constantly darting, your speech more honest
than poetry—how you focus the world
we walk in. Instead, I keep
my eyes on the page.

Spareribs

For hours they simmered in the flame-
covered enameled cast iron casserole—steeping
walls and cabinets, even yellow-patterned formica—
in the scent of meat relaxing its grip on the bone.

When we had covered the picnic table
with the red-checked cloth, placed
china plates and cutlery, poured homemade
lemonade, tart and gritty with undissolved

sugar, mother brought out the steaming pot.
We joined hands and lowered our eyes
to the jacquard pattern of daisies woven into
the white squares. Then she opened the lid

to let out the steam, reached into the pot
and spooned out ribs, amber juices dripping onto
our lifted plates. I sucked the marrow
from the cut ends of meat-padded bones.

Today I order ribs in a restaurant (rarely)
where the checkered tablecloths are plastic,
where I am served impostors lathered
in bottled barbecue sauce, too strong

and too sweet, fat partly congealed, meat tough
and feisty, nothing like the melting flavor
of those served on the slope of our weedy back yard
where we picked clover blossoms with our bare toes

under the table, where the distant hum of traffic
soothed us, in the days when I never considered
what it cost my mother to create the feeling that we
would be sitting there together for the rest of our lives.

Apparition

It's early morning before work
and I'm chasing my toddler
across the unraked yard when all of a sudden
my father's canvas-covered shoulders appear to rise
from among the scattered leaves.
He looms statuesque in the midst of the lawn
like Hamlet's ghost, brown wool hat
shading his eyes and beak-like nose.
I didn't see him coming and now
for a few inscrutable moments
the river of years between us carves
a ravine so deep I fear
he has already moved on over to the other side.
I forget he was born to this season
when yellow leaves or few or none do hang
upon those boughs . . . that every year since I saw
him blow out forty shining candles on a chocolate cake
I have breathed an autumn prayer against his loss.
Yet he has watched over me
for forty years since.
His shoulder is warm beneath my palm
and a slow grin cracks his face as
his youthful miniature tugs his pant leg,
pulling him towards the house they are building
next door, telling Opa all about men hammering
and pouring concrete.

Unspoken

A fine storyteller, he used the pauses well—
especially when it came to his own life.
He kept us guessing at important things.

"Among the Amish, *Thank you* is only said
to strangers," he once said. Now we measure
his silence at the other end of the phone line

wondering how much he knows, how much
he infers from all the doctor's visits, our careful
questions. As a girl I listened with my sisters

as he suspended us from a thread
of language, reading from *The Best-Loved
Poems of the American People* a rhyme

about three silly women sailing over
a waterfall in a tin washtub.
Now in the whirlpool

at my vacation cabin he tells
us girls that it has all slipped
away so fast. I look out the window

to a fine dusting of snow. The cold
world on the other side of the glass
reminds me of tales he's told about hunting,

waiting for hours in a quiet wood,
the deer an excuse for listening
and sitting still. It reminds me of

the silence of his long afternoon
naps. The quiet as he clicked typewriter
keys on the other side of his closed office door.

We sit together now as the jets pump the swirling
hot water around us, its steam rising to fog
our glasses, disguise our tears.

When I Came Home from College

I didn't want to visit friends. Leaving behind the realms
of ambiguity and abstraction, all I wanted was to stay
in mother's laundry room with its ordered shelves
and shiny enameled machines, to inhale steam
from the iron or the lavender scent
of moist spray- starched collars
as I pressed my father's shirts.
Every morning the sun rose to the freshly
brewing coffee, followed by the comforting routines
of toast-making and table-clearing;
hot breath of the dishwasher cleansing my pores,
dry glassware slightly resisting my touch
as I placed items on papered shelves.
Soon we had lunch, then took a walk or a swim
before chopping onions at four for dinner at six,
father's step on the creaking stair coinciding with the hour.
After supper I sat in a lawn chair on the front porch
with my mother; as the music of my younger sisters'
voices rose from the lawn, her gentle
speech reordered the world, stars grew close
and familiar as light filling the cracks
of a dark worn shade pulled for an afternoon nap.

Collectors

"He likes the dark ones,"
my Aunt Lizzie explained
when the collector turned down
her quilts; we unfolded them between us
in her scrubbed kitchen, admired the stitching.
In the afternoon shadow shiny scraps
of polyester caught my eye.

Ignorant of the axiom of quilts—
they're made of what's at hand—I
tugged at my mother's sleeve
and whispered, "Doesn't she know
that natural fibers are her tradition?
That wool and cotton are better?"

Now I browse through coffee-table
books whose pages celebrate the art
of anonymous women in impeccably printed
photo reproductions. Aunt Lizzie is too old
and arthritic to piece (although Uncle
Sammie still cuts and sews). Though she changed
her patterns and bought cotton remnants
machine-dyed in the old dark colors,
she never let a camera into her house.

I wait till the price of the book
goes down so I can pick up a bargain
like Aunt Lizzie picked out remnants,
too thrifty to pay good money for fabrics
that wouldn't need much wear.

Retirement

The simple patterns of a day
at my parents' home now:
sounds of washing in the bathroom,
mother in her robe making coffee,
rubbing her eyes, searching for her glasses.
Father searching for a pan,
measuring water,
stirring oatmeal for one.
Mother sits, her feet resting on a chair,
its finish worn by use, drinks
half her juice, saves the rest.
After breakfast, cleaning dishes,
both rest: father in his bed,
mother on three kitchen chairs
aligned to hold her weight.
They read or write
in separate rooms till nearly noon.
Mother may go for groceries,
father to the post office;
she sets out lunch, heats soup,
they eat, clean up,
and rest again.
Afternoons may hold
appointments, errands, swimming at the Y,
or, in rarer moments, more reading
and some laundry. At four
dinner preparation begins.
Mother's chore. At five-thirty
father appears like clockwork
ready to eat. They sit to table, say grace,
eat, clean up, then watch the news
and rest. Perhaps they talk
to their grown children

on the phone, write letters,
watch ice hockey on TV.
It's bedtime and they rest again,
sorting through the memories
that circulate within their blood,
their minds, heavy with a lifetime's
work, care, love.

Kitchen Sink Meditation; or,
Ode to the One I Refused

Sometimes the dishcloth at my sink
releases the sweet antiseptic pungency
of fifty children cared for in their metal cribs
at the Mount Vernon State Home
for the mentally retarded where once I joined
the Christian kids and Kevin with his bushy red beard
and guitar on Sunday afternoons
to entertain the ones that no one
wanted, few visited, where alarmed steel
and glass doors opened onto empty puce
linoleum hallways—probably asbestos—
polished chemical clean
with a lingering aftertaste sweet as the voice
of the lipsticked social worker who smiled
and explained at us as though we were too dumb
to question her goodness.

One little girl—whose name I can't
remember—her too-light frame resting on my hip,
locked around me like a cage of bone when I had to leave.
I pried apart her tightly laced fingers and ankles
crossed forcefully as knives, her silently shaking
body, from my own. All week she haunted me—
she was little more than two and her parents
hadn't visited for months, a nurse had told me
when I'd asked. Some of the kids had photos
or greeting cards taped to the rectangular steel bars
of their beds. Her bars were blank and smooth.
The pain I imagined for her was a splinter
in my own well-paced and cared-for heart,
so full of complicated family feelings

at a distance, a distance I had chosen—
it was my freshman year of college—from my parents
who loved, or at least (I thought then) hovered over me
too well.

All week I adopted her,
over and over her hollow little dark face
peered through my dreams, the skin
of her neck against my nose sweeter
than the scent or urine and fear she lived in.
But where could she sleep in my narrow single
dorm room? How could I carry her with me to classes?
What would she do all day when I left her alone?

Perhaps I could bring her pictures, mobiles,
a music box. The gray empty light of November
Sunday afternoons filled me with dread.
I felt too sick to board the yellow school bus,
to breathe the empty sweetness of scrubbed hallways.
After all, I could never adopt her, I reasoned.
My parents were paying good money
to send me to college, not her.
All *they* needed was an extra child.
I would become just another Sunday visitor
who would eventually abandon her.
So when Sunday came around again
and Kevin hoisted his guitar
into the van, Tom put on his clown of God
face, and Maeve pulled her long pale hair
from the collar of her charcoal coat
with her pink-nailed hands,
I stayed in my room.

Senior year as I returned my books to the library desk
one final time, the student on duty recalled

to me how Maeve had made a study of one
of the children from the home—now closed down—
measuring the effects of visual and aural stimulation
on intellectual growth. Her subject
had made terrific progress—in what? I wondered.
Developing enough intelligence to feel her loss
more keenly?—but when the project was over
slid back into the non-responsive womb
of her crib.

Now as I try to scrub and spray the smell
of decaying organic matter, of antiseptic-sweetened
molds from my kitchen sink, I think
of how many times I've done, will do, this task.
My daughter passes through, her Barbie-filled arms
moving her collection to another room.

Training

When my little sister had her violin lessons
twice a week with the retired Russian master,
I didn't know that when he closed the door
behind her she would play her scales beautifully
for him and he would reward her by trying
to thrust his bulky old man's tongue
into her small resisting mouth or
brush her barely budded breasts
with his trained fingers. Waiting
for her outside in the chintz-covered chairs,
leafing through *Life* or *Time* or *Ebony*
in the music school's parlor, I didn't know
that behind the heavy oak door in room two
my sister was keeping her teeth braced,
determined to practice whether or where
her teacher touched her.
Years later, as she performs the delicate
Baroque ornaments of Biber and Vivaldi
I listen. She plays before us
in a sweeping blue satin dress she has sewn herself,
nodding at the harpsichordist,
smiling at the sounds they create together.
I run again and again
to a heavy oak door, pounding till my fists
are bruised, till an ancient man opens
and I gaze past him into
an empty room. My sister?
She was released ages ago.
Standing before me,
in blue satin,
she bows to sustained applause.

The Art Student

for Peggy

She drew old women—lines of their faces
fanning out across the page—transferred
them onto huge linoleum blocks and cut
the wrinkles with thousands of slices, creating
a web-like pattern against the dark background.

At the college art show students and parents couldn't
get enough of the crones she cut and printed
on sheets of rice paper, they looked so real.
But her teachers judged her unimaginative,
derivative, because she used photographs. She kept on

with the old-lady portraits, her long dark curls
tied back with a scarf, sketching at breakfast
after staying up all night, living on Tab,
Snickers, and insulin. One night she walked
with me in the dark after we'd painted portraits

of the "Thalidomide Kid," props for some play we never saw,
scent of turpentine still lingering in our skin as
we wandered the lanes of rural Ohio lit only by sky, till
we thought we had joined its boundless constellations,
till Peggy clutched my arm and said, "I don't know

if I can make it home." Back inside the dorm
she madly prodded the vending machine, stripped
the wrapper from the lumpy chocolate, sat on the steps
and ate. She told me she could eat the candy if she drank
the diet stuff. All through that year she was my guide

to a maze of men and parties, the realms of possibility
in lack of sleep, stretching her limits in homage

to an inner martinet. Playing daily with her time
and chemistry she hoped to eke out time enough
to finish the "ladies" she'd started. The art

department was giving her grief, she said. Damn it,
she could draw. So what if she used photographs?
Her last work, a delicate dry point of two tiny women
leaning on each other in the space of a sheet of Arches
she sold out before she had finished pulling the edition.

The Saturday morning after her mysterious death—
she was found locked in her single, unconscious next to a half-
opened candy bar, empty insulin bottles scattered everywhere.
After a week on the respirator she was given up by her family—
the printmaking professor and I finished pulling the edition

in the empty basement in three hours of complete silence.
Gradually I gave up art that year. I saw how
much it cost to forge a vision of one's own, how
in every print Peggy was dying a little more. At least
in her last print, I thought, two women stood together.

Examination

For Kevin Leiske, May 1996

Hunched over the metal and formica desk
like so many others in the gym, you sit
in the front row, head bowed,
writing and thinking. How like a child
in spite of your football player's size.
Your close-cropped hair is teddy bear brown,
long lashes, child-like, veil your sea-blue eyes,
even your Jimmy Buffet *Treasures* t-shirt
is faded to a favorite blanket's
often-washed pastel.

He was the kind of guy
who threw the block parties
everyone came to, who played
Jimmy Buffet till the wee hours,
They said about your dad.
He came to every hockey game,
adopted your teammates
as his sons. At home
you were his only one.

Buffet albums and model planes
stood before the closed casket
at his wake where I scrutinized
a collage of photographs
for traces of you in his healthy
grinning pilot's face. I found you
and our arms reached round each other
tight. I couldn't find the words.

Now, several weeks later, moving in
a void your friends and teachers can barely

imagine, you work your way
through the test, item by item—
with your own words, in your own time.
Your brown jacket droops
from the rounded shoulders of the plastic
folding chair as your own strong
shoulders rise firmly through t-shirt cotton
as you guide the blue tip
of your pilot pen across the page.

Medicine Woman

for Kayt Havens

She searches for new ways
to heal herself and others—listens
to the rain and wind, to her own heartbeat,
its complicated yearnings. Driving
the family mini-van to work she looks out
through a rain-spattered windshield
onto city streets as the taped voice of another woman
tells the story of a Navaho code talker imprisoned, tortured,
and released to a veteran's hospital. *He could not walk*
for a year and so he went home to see his people
for one last time. The tribe gathered
to watch him crawl across hard ground.
The elders took his crutches, threw him
into deep water, instructed him to call
his spirit back or follow it
to another world. She still remembers
the story when she sits under the fluorescent
lights of her office in the hospital across
from a young girl who bears the ripening
fruit of unprotected sex. She wonders
how to call her spirit back.

After T'ao Chi'en
I couldn't want another life. This is my
true calling, working with students and my own children,

using the little I've learned in life to teach them.
Faithfully, I work every day, and yet

there's always failure: thoughtless words,
misunderstandings, ungraded papers, and unwashed clothes.

I'm not asking for more than a task I can do
well, a living that will support my family,

but it's a struggle just to get the kids
to school on time, to begin a lesson for my students

promptly. Oh, it can leave me stricken
with grief when I think of my own

poems unwritten, drawings not drawn.
That's how it is.

Nothing can change it. But then,
I'll delight in a smile, a word well-used,

a student's thanks, a child's hug, a paper well-written,
an image recorded, my scratchings on this page.

BOOK FOUR

Exhibitions

Rules of the Game

Bone.
Hey Bone.
Bone.
Yeah Bone.
Booooooooone.
Boys in class
bubble with language
but bounce
only one word
at a time across the room
like a basketball thunk thunk thunk
Shoooot
or a drumbeat pounded
on a taut hide playing with
its echo. *Bone.*
Bone.
       Bone.
Bone.
These guys
don't dress up
for Halloween:
their helmets, hockey pads,
jockstraps, jackets, and ties
are real now.
When God
handed out testosterone
he surely spilled the jar
right where they were standing.
The other students
watch and wait
to see what I will call
in the game
of verbal basketball.

Surge

A soda explodes from the swollen shaken can
as five large boys leap towards two teachers
in the classroom doorway—overturning
tables and chairs, legs and bolts flying
everywhere sprinkled with ejaculatory fizz.
And then it's over.
They stand breathless, laughing a little,
foam of the moment subsiding and we
two teachers stand terrified
by a random display of force
we don't understand in the last sacred space
in America: the classroom.
My colleague, a gray-bearded Aikido master,
leaves in search of a disciplinarian,
while I wait with the now-sheepish boys.
Jay's shoulder-length hair drapes over
his massive shoulders like that of the fat girl
shamed and vindictive before her classmates.
Ike's dark muscular football captain's body
folds in on itself like that of a five-year-old.
Joe's elegant rebellious profile turns
from me, lumberjack shoulders shielding
his privacy. Ian's small, sharp face
resumes its surprised, scholarly look
behind his steel-rimmed glasses, beneath
the roof-peak thatch of his hair, its purple dye
fading. Rob dissolves into a shadow, if
shadows can be chrysanthemum pink.
"We saw it on TV," Jay pleads.
But I am clueless. I don't watch TV.
His comment only conjures for me
the reels of re-runs that must spin endlessly behind
his eye-sockets, between his ears.

What else could prompt five senior boys
about to graduate to confuse imagination
with reality? My colleague returns
with the oldest male teacher he can find—
an elder whose voice still carries authority,
whose attention the boys have earned.

He holds them after school in a room
with closed door. When he releases them
they march silent and blushing
past my open office door.
At home, my own kids tell me, "Mom,
it's only a commercial
in which the kids would do anything
to get to the *Surge.*"

My Sister's Report Card

When my younger sister turned five
I decided I'd learn to ride a bike
by teaching her how. I'd pass on all
of the instructions I'd been given
that I hadn't managed to follow,
hoping she'd make a success
of it. I watched her pedal her training wheels
up and down the sidewalk, streamers flying
to meet the tips of her blond braids,
the striped skirt of the seersucker dress my mother had
sewed her billowing beneath her (I had a twin dress
just like it in my closet I felt too old to wear)
and checked off the categories
of the report card I'd made her, something
I could do now that I had learned
to read and write. Finally our father
joined her, running up and down the walk
with his hand on the rear tire till
she took off on her own. I gave her
an "A" and handed her the card
she still couldn't read. Every night afterwards
I dreamed that suddenly I was doing
it too, balancing between the wheels,
flying down the alley in the way
that seemed to come so naturally
to others, releasing the fear
that kept me firmly planted on the earth.

Priestess of Love

I wanted to be a priestess of love,
angel of mercy, crystal in a sun-streaked window
staining the world, a dark red valentine pressed
between the pages of a schoolboy's book, an obscure
poem about water, wind, stone, heat
of sun on rock, a musk-scented grove of fern.
Instead I drew psychedelic patterns
on my toes with colored marker and flaunted
them through my leather thongs
at my best friend's older brother
when he took us in his yellow mustang to hear the burning
cool flute of Herbie Mann. I wanted
to cover myself with paint and roll on canvas,
make art with the instrument I loved the best,
my virginal body with its swelling breasts,
twin pelvic bones delicately protruding on either side
of my barely risen belly. Like the moist,
searching tongue of a deer stripping bark
from a sapling I thirsted for the world,
like tiny bubbles in champagne
I rose and crested,
waiting to overflow.

Teacher's Dream

When they handed me the baby
his open mouth clotted with macaroni
and cheese—the soft buttery kind they serve
in school cafeterias—his gums were already ridged
with teeth. How could I nurse him?
You don't need to feed him, my husband said.
I've just made him some nice macaroni and cheese.
Take a rest. Suddenly I feel the pressure
of milk in my full breasts. I don't have to
give it to anyone.

I must feed them, I think,
when my students appear at the appointed hour,
their notebooks full of poems.
But I am wrong again. They are already full.
All I need to do is help them set the table
for their own feasts, find some common dishes
we can pass. I clamp my arms hard against
my own leaking.

Signifiers

After returning home
from a day filled with letters

and numbers, crafting comments
for parents and reducing students' efforts

to pairs of digits, I draw a hot bath and slip
into the tub only to find numbers and letters

floating in the water about me: the bright
colored plastics of my daughter's bath toys.

Yoga with Rose

Back pressed against the tough library carpet,
I close my eyes and listen to the voice
that persuades me I am lying on a sandy beach,
limbs grown heavy and warmed by sun,
weight of my flesh absorbed by the ground.
The scent of graham crackers hovers
just above the floor as I crack my eyes
to see the other teachers lying in the circle,
feet towards the candle in the center
of the darkened room. If I listen
closely, I can hear the autumn wind rattle
the skylight, rain preparing to fall.
After the class Rose will open a shoe box
and offer us muffins she baked herself,
pour brewed Mango Ceylon tea into styrofoam
cups. Now she pauses to flip the stopped
cassette and presses the button to resume
the whispered chimes of mood music.
How I long to hover here forever
in the shelter of our adult naptime.

BOOK FIVE

En Plein Air

Ministry

After hearing the organ and the choir
at St. Paul's Episcopal, I filled
out the visitor's card in the rack
on the back of the pew.

A few days later I receive
an evening phone call.
"Who are you?" the priest asks.
What do you want?

No one ever fills out those cards."
Deep breath.
I want you to know I was there,
a soul on a journey

who slipped alone into your sanctuary
space. I thought I could fill out a card
as thanks, to let you know someone
had worshipped in this place.

The Burden

I set the table and they come,
bringing books and backpacks,
thick china plates piled with french fries,
burgers, pasta, bowls of apple jacks,
poems they've folded and stashed
in their pockets, journals they've filled
with looped rows of words, cut-out pictures,
drawings, lyrics from treasured songs,
visions and fears and angers
not wanted elsewhere.

For weeks I urge them to find
their voices, bare
their souls, ask them to ponder
the meaning of their lives; then,
when they have done it, I carry
their papers with me unread
for weeks, a burden too heavy for
a mere English teacher.

Finally I lift the pages of the first, then second,
read slowly for hours, absorbing their courage,
their chaos, phrases they've wrenched from mind
into language. I remember how, when I was a child,
I'd bundle my unsorted prayers off to God
in a laundry-sized sack. Was this how
she felt when she opened them and tried
to sort out what I'd meant to say?

Forty-Something in Milwaukee

Sitting alone at a bar
for the first time in almost twenty
years I sip my Sprecher quickly and avoid
the gaze of the only other customer, a brooding
overweight man in a sport jacket, turning my eyes
to the wall that sports reproductions of Victorian floozies
smoking or removing their garters, then back to the bartender,
a woman about my age in a velvet hat with gold trim.
Excuses for my solitude rise to my lips:
"The others didn't show . . .
"My husband's working late . . .
"I had a sitter anyway and didn't want to waste her . . ."
She puts on a CD video—Eric Clapton,
Unplugged—my babysitter's music,
and I find a place to rest my eyes:
Clapton's fingers on the neck of an acoustic
guitar, unplugged, I get it . . .
the same musician who disturbed
my fourteen-year-old radio-headphone nights
with his lustful Cream electric acid rock
plays earnestly, quietly, seated,
hair and beard trimmed, like a college professor
on anti-depressants, someone who has lasted
through a lot. "Not a bad cut on this CD,"
says a thirty-ish young man who's slid
up to the bar with his big-haired girlfriend.
My eyes on Clapton's face, his eyes closed
behind horn-rimmed glasses, I order another
Sprecher as he launches into "Hey, hey . . ."
the beer now an excuse to linger
at the edge of the padded formica semi-circle
till he breaks into *Tears in Heaven*.
"Getting to be a popular song at funerals,"

the gregarious young man says.
"He's a funeral director," the girlfriend nods.
"That's how come he knows."
"I hope you're wearing that hat in heaven,"
he tells the bartender.
I must be invisible . . . Clapton sings.
The brooding man pays his tab and leaves.
The sweat-beaded glass turns again and again
in my fingers. Sinking into the tank
of my loneliness, clinging to the edge
of a circle no one else perceives,
I pay my tab and go, pausing to watch
the speckled fish pacing the aquarium
set into the opposite wall, an albino frog
trying to disturb their steady routine,
his tiny helpless arms clawing
the water near his unseeing head,
pink legs and delicately webbed feet
propelling him again and again
on his futile journey.

Insomnia

Lying awake in the hotel bed
I find in my breathing
an empty space, a square
of light or air, thin air,
into which for years
I've feared to fall.
A crawling infant refusing
to cross a glass-covered hole
in a patterned floor, I have been
arrested by my terror.
Opening my eyes in the dark
I am a hollow chocolate rabbit,
a ceramic doll like the one I chose for my seventh
birthday, her limbs held to her fragile body
by elastic strings crisscrossed
through her vacant core.
I let the darkness rush into me,
imagine the hunger I still feel
when sated. A dreamer
habitually courting sleep, I hurl
myself down this precipice,
startled into wonder
that I am still lying in my bed,
that I am holding
myself as I fall.

Night Vigil

"Disorder is the order we are not looking for." —*Henri Bergson*

Washing congealed chocolate frosting
off stoneware saucers at 2:00 a.m. while
reinstalling software on the computer, hoping
to resolve an incompatibility,
I navigate the night kitchen
through the debris my vacationing family
has left behind: a Swiss Army knife nestled
between the open pages of a cookbook
next to two Christmas stockings, opened
cards in a red and green basket, patient
hubbard and acorn squash waiting
for weeks to be cut or steamed or pureed
into soup, my husband's tie looped
across a pile of books and catalogs
at one end of the kitchen island.
Calmly I load the dishwasher, wipe
down counters, unhurried as in a dream
where my limbs are leaden, stuff
the corners of trash cans already overflowing
with empty cartons and table scraps.
The computer runs out of memory,
then loses its face as I restart it over
and over; after 2:39 a.m. time begins to flow
backwards, each step saved reverts
to miles of lost time. Across the room
I catch the title of an abandoned paperback:
Who Do You Think You Are?

Solitaire

When she retreated to her bedroom
for weeks, Mrs. V passed the time
with solitaire. I know, because once
I tiptoed into the dusty room where
the pickled odor of Scotch rose to crush
my breath, where rosaries and nylon underwear
spilled out of curved mahogany drawers,
where Christ opened his flaming heart
to us from his framed perch on the wall
across from the bed where the worn
cards were laid out in neat piles.

In my family cards were viewed
as such a waste of time that nobody
even knew how to play. They fit perfectly
into the equation with idols and alcohol,
trinkets that substituted for prayers.
But even in her drunken ravings—
the ones that wafted across her lawn to ours
summer evenings before I said my prayers—
Christ was watching Mrs. V; perhaps
she was even calling out to him.

While she waited for the demon
to seize her with its voice, she'd cleverly
play hour after hour—a game of arrangement
and chance—a game her daughter
taught me when we took her with us
to the beach. Years later, late at night,
alone, waiting for a poem to come, I remember
Mrs. V, her daughter who shared my name,
as I deal again and again at the computer
screen, waiting for that winning hand.

On her good days she'd descend the stairs
in her slippers, peach nightgown swaying against
her mottled blue shins. She'd read
to us from Little Women, help us plan
the play we'd been writing from our favorite book.
She'd wanted to be an actress, and her readings
of Jo made us wonder how she'd missed
the silver screen. She gave us spaghetti-strap
gowns of taffeta and tulle, even her floor-length
wedding veil trailing from a sequined cap,
which we wore when marching up and down the block.

One Christmas eve I stayed with her youngest son
while her husband took the other children to midnight
mass. We watched the blazing lights of the ornament-
laden tree, strains of Mel Torme filling up the room, keeping
her rantings far away. "Don't be afraid of her.
She won't come down," he reassured me. When at last
he fell asleep, his head on my knee, I listened to her curse
her husband, her kids, the demons that kept her
imprisoned in the high tower of her bedroom,
locked in a rage against the truth
of solitaire: some hands you're dealt
will not play out.

Journey

Don't touch me. Just listen to the rain.
Lying beside you I open my pores
to the sound of rain, the breath of rain,
the round voice of rain expanding and contracting
in the lung of the ear. I think of my mother
breathing cleanly and deeply under the oxygen tent,
her first sound sleep in weeks. Rain washes
every half-formed thought from my mind,
leaf-clogged gutters sluiced with rushing
water, fluid washed from her lungs
by diuretics, my mother grateful, finally
for the adjustable hospital bed, nurses' attention,
a schedule managed by someone else.
I breathe in the scent of rain
until my ears are soaked with the sense
of her breathing. Then, at last, I can offer
my body to your hands. Your caresses
lead me into a cherished house whose moldings
and doorframes, tables, benches, and picture frames
are of a deeply grained wood polished by years
of human touch. Into a gentle woods
whose wet bare trees are still surrounded
by auras of color. I walk through room
after room, path after path of matted leaves,
image after image of cherished objects
I have longed for, have ached to own, to touch.
As you enter me, I enter the image
of yet another doorframe opening
onto yet another. You walk through me over
and over as I journey through you
to familiar landscapes
I have never seen before.

The Author

Ann Hostetler was born in Mt. Pleasant, Pennsylvania and grew up in Scottdale, Pennsylvania and Alberta, Canada. Her family settled in the greater Philadelphia area when she was eight years old. Traveling back and forth with her families between the geographies of Pennsylvania and western Canada, spending summers with Amish relatives, and accompanying her family on travels to Amish and Hutterite communities as her father did field work for several anthropological studies, helped form her thinking.

Ann attended Kenyon College in Gambier, Ohio, where she received a degree in studio art. After working in New York City and Philadelphia in publishing for several years, Ann went on to study English literature at Pennsylvania State University, where she received an M.A., and at the University of Pennsylvania, where she received a Ph.D. Throughout her studies, Ann continued to write poetry, a love she developed in grade school, and her work reflects the influence of her studies in art and literature as well as her devotion to family life and her love of nature.

Ann teaches English and creative writing at Goshen College in Indiana, where she lives with her husband Merv Smucker and their four children. She has also taught at the University of Wisconsin-Milwaukee, Marquette University, and the University School of Milwaukee. She has edited an anthology of poetry by writers from Mennonite contexts, *A Capella: Mennonite Voices in Poetry*, and has published on contemporary poetry and fiction in a variety of journals. Her poetry has appeared in *The American Scholar*, *The Cream City Review*, *The Mid-America Poetry Review*, *Mothering*, and *The Mennonite*, among other places.